A gift from
Wisconsin Evangelical Lutheran Synod
Prison Ministry
P.O. Box 452
New Ulm, MN 56073

I am Blessed through God's Word

A self-study course about how a Christian is blessed through the study of God's Word

Multi-Language Publications
Bringing the Written Word to the World

This book is dedicated to the Reverend Harold A. Essmann, who in 1996 was the founder of the Multi-Language Publications program.

The text for this book is prepared by Multi-Language Publications of the Board for World Missions of the Wisconsin Evangelical Lutheran Synod.

Copyright © 2012

Printed in 2012

ISBN 978-1-931891-30-1

The colored cover picture is the work of Glenn Myers. Other black and white pictures are the work of Glenn Myers. Glenn Myers' illustrations are reserved by Northwestern Publishing House.

Scripture is taken from the Holy Bible, New International Reader's Version.
Copyright © 1996, 1998 by the International Bible Society, Used by permission of the International Bible Society.

Book 24

Table of Contents

Getting Started 1

Chapter 1 - God's Word
   is true and a guide in my life 3

Chapter 2 - God's Word
   reminds me that I am a sinner 15

Chapter 3 - God's Word
   shows me God's love 29

Chapter 4 - God's Word
   blesses me in my life on earth 43

Chapter 5 - God's Word
   guides and helps me during days of suffering 63

Chapter 6 - God's Word
   leads me to eternal life in heaven 77

Word List 93

Answers to Chapter Tests 97

Final Test 99

Getting Started

The purpose of these lessons is to show you how you are blessed as a believer, as a Christian. You are blessed in many ways through God's Word.

Each of the six chapters begins with a list of goals marked with a small star (*). These goals will tell you what you will be learning in that chapter. There will be a few questions after each section, and a short test at the end of each chapter. If you read each section carefully, you should be able to answer the questions correctly without much trouble.

At the end of each group of questions and at the end of each chapter you will be given a page number to which you can turn to check your answers. Check your answers carefully, correcting any mistakes. Make sure you understand the answers before reading on any further.

At the end of each chapter there are Bible references that you should read. In these Bible references you can find further evidence of what is taught in the lesson. We want you to be sure that what this course is teaching is exactly what the Bible teaches.

At the end of the book there is a final test. Before you begin answering the questions in this final test, go back and review the chapter tests. When you have completed the final test, you can either give the test to the person who gave you this book or mail it to the address found on the back cover of this book.

You may order other books to read or to study.

God bless you in the study of his Word that brings many blessings to you in your life.

2

Mary listens to God's Word - Luke 10:38-42

Chapter One

God's Word is true and a guide in my life

When I was a young boy, I delivered newspapers from door to door each evening. In the middle of winter when it was dark outside and people had light in their homes, I would deliver a newspaper to an elderly husband and wife who lived across the street from my home. I remember that I could look through the window of their home and see them at their table after they were finished with eating their evening meal. I could see the man reading from a large open Bible. That scene of a husband and wife reading and listening to God's Word from a Bible made such a great impression on me that I can recall it today some 70 or more years later.

4

Why do people read God's Word? Why is reading God's Word so important in a Christian's life today? In this chapter we learn that God's Word is true and a guide in our lives.

> * God's Word is inspired by God and is without errors, and

> * God's Word is very powerful showing me my sin and my Savior.

God's Word, the Bible, is important! Through the Bible God speaks to you and me personally. God uses many men and women to bring his Word to us. I can think of men like Moses in the Old Testament who records the Ten Commandments in Exodus chapter 20; or of Isaiah, the prophet, who lived 700 years before the birth of Jesus. Isaiah writes about the sufferings of Jesus in Isaiah chapter 53.

Then there are books in the Bible about women such as Ruth, who is an ancestor of Jesus, and Esther, who saves her people from destruction. King David writes many of the Psalms. His son, King Solomon, writes the book of Proverbs. In the New Testament God speaks to us through men like Matthew, Mark, Luke, and John as well as the apostle Paul.

But it is God who breathes into these people the very words and thoughts to write. God the Holy Spirit guides them. Consider what the apostle Peter writes: "Above all, here is what you must understand. No prophecy in Scripture ever came from a prophet's own understanding. It never came simply because a prophet wanted it to. Instead, the Holy Spirit guided the prophets as they spoke. So prophecy comes from God" (2 Peter 1:20,21). The apostle Paul also writes: "We never stop thanking God for the way you received his word. You heard it from us. But you didn't accept it as a human word. You accepted it for what it really is. It is God's word" (1 Thessalonians 2:13). Therefore, it is God who speaks to you and me in the Bible. The Bible is God's Word.

1. The Bible is _____ Word.

2. Through the Bible, God speaks to _____ and me.

3. Isaiah writes about the sufferings of _____.

4. It is God who breathes into these people the very _____ and _____ to write.

5. It is God himself who _____ to you and me in the Bible.

(Answers to these questions are found on page 11)

There are no mistakes in God's Word. The Bible is true in all that I read and learn. Moses, the great prophet of God, writes, "God isn't a mere man. He cannot lie" (Numbers 23:19). Above all Jesus, God's Son, tells me in his prayer to God the Father: "Your word is truth" (John 17:17).

I know that God is very powerful. God's Word also is very powerful. The apostle Paul reminds me of this when he writes, "I am not ashamed of the good news. It is God's power. And it will save everyone who believes. It is meant first of all for the Jews. It is meant also for those who are not Jews" (Romans 1:16). This means that the Bible is written for all people. These words written by the apostle Paul at God's direction are very important to me. They tell me, first of all, that the "good news," or the news about my Savior, or the "gospel," is God's power. The central teaching of the gospel is that God sent his Son, Jesus Christ, to be our Savior. Jesus, God's Son, came into this world when he was conceived by the Holy Spirit in the virgin Mary. He is both true God and true man. As the God-man, he lived under God's law and kept it perfectly for me because I cannot keep it perfectly. God orders me to keep his law perfectly when he tells me, "Be perfect as your Father in heaven is perfect" (Matthew 5:48).

But I was born in sin and I commit sins every day. I cannot keep God's law perfectly. Jesus, as the sinless Son of God, kept God's law for me. As both God and man Jesus was born in the world to bear the punishment for my sins. I deserve to die. The Bible tells me, "When you sin, the pay you get is death" (Romans 6:23). This pay is not only death at the end of my life on earth, but also eternal death in hell, eternal separation from a loving God. But the apostle Paul also brings me good news in Romans 6:23 when he writes, "But God gives you the gift of eternal life because of what Christ Jesus our Lord has done."

6. The Bible is written for _____ people.

7. I cannot keep God's law _____.

8. I was born in _____ and commit _____ every day.

9. Jesus, as the sinless Son of God, kept God's _____ for me.

10. Because we sin, the payment we should receive is _____.

11. God gives us the gift of _____ _____ because of what Christ Jesus our Lord has done.

(Answers to these questions are found on page 11)

What did Christ Jesus, our Lord, do for me? He not only kept God's law perfectly for me, but Jesus also was punished for my sins when he died for me on the cross and then rose from death. God tells me in the Bible, "Jesus was handed over to die for our sins. He was raised to life in order to make us right with God" (Romans 4:25). Jesus is my Savior from sin, death and hell.

12. Jesus kept God's law for me _____.

13. Jesus also was punished for my _____ when he died for me on the _____.

14. Jesus is my _____.

(Answers to these questions are found on page 11)

This message from God's Word fills my heart with joy. God is my loving Maker and Jesus is my loving Savior. Now I want to learn more about how God saves me through what Jesus did for me. There are many ways I can do this.

- I can read the Bible to learn about God's love for me through Jesus.
- I can study the Bible together with others to understand God's message about Jesus.
- I can worship Jesus in my church.
- I can sing hymns of praise to Jesus.
- I can live a Christian life to honor Jesus.

Jesus, Shepherd of the sheep,
Who your Father's flock does keep,
Safe we wake and safe we sleep,
Guarded still by you.

By your blood our souls were bought;
By your life salvation wrought;
By your light our feet are taught,
Lord, to follow you. (CW 436)

Review of Chapter One

It is God who breathed the thoughts and very words into men he chose to write his Word, that is, the Bible. Some of these men are the prophets of the Old Testament. Others who wrote God's Word are the Gospel writers and apostles of the New Testament.

Everything I read in the Bible is God's Word and it is without any errors. The two main teachings of the Bible are God's law and the good news also known as the gospel. The Word of God is very powerful in our lives. It shows me that I am born in sin and commit sins every day. Because of my sin I deserve to die, not only at the end of my life on earth, but also eternally in hell. However, in love God shows me my Savior, Jesus Christ. As both true God and true man, Jesus kept God's law for me perfectly. Jesus also was punished for everyone's sins when he died on the cross. God was satisfied with Jesus' deeds and raised him from the dead.

This message of God's law and the gospel fills my heart with joy, and I want to study God's Word and worship Jesus for what he has done. I praise God with the spiritual songs that I sing and the Christian life that I live.

Answers to the questions in Chapter One:
1. God's; 2. you; 3. Jesus; 4. words, thoughts; 5. speaks; 6. all; 7. perfectly; 8. sin, sins; 9. law; 10. death; 11. eternal, life; 12. perfectly; 13. sins, cross; 14. Savior.

Chapter One Test

1. The Bible is _____ Word.

2. It is God himself who _____ to you and me in the Bible.

3. The Bible was written for _____ people.

4. I cannot keep God's law _____.

5. Jesus, as the sinless Son of God, kept God's _____ for me perfectly.

6. Jesus was punished for my _____ when he died for me on the _____.

7. Jesus is my _____.

8. Write some ways you learn more about Jesus.
   _____
   _____
   _____
   _____

(Answers to these questions are found on page 97)

Read how people of the Bible learned more about their Savior:

Luke 10:38-42 – Jesus teaches Mary.

Acts 17:10-12 – The people in the city of Berea studied God's Word.

14

Moses and the Ten Commandments - Exodus 32:15-19

Chapter Two

God's Word reminds me that I am a sinner

When I was much younger than I am now, I belonged to a mission society. One of my duties was to visit the prison in the city where I lived. I would visit the prison once a week and meet with some of the prisoners. I still remember the bad feelings I had when the guards in the prison closed the iron barred doors behind me, and I would find myself in the hall which was lined with prison cells. A question that any visitor there might ask is WHY? Why were these people in prison? The answer is simple. They were in prison because they broke the law. Some of the prisoners stole. Some had hurt or even killed other people.

In the same way I am a prisoner. I also break laws. I break the laws of God. As a result I become a prisoner of my own evil nature as well as the prisoner of the devil. In the end, unless I learn otherwise, I will be held forever in the prison of hell.

In this chapter we learn:

> * God's Word reminds me that I am a sinner, and

> * How sin affects me in my life.

Why is sin so much a part of our lives? Where does sin come from? God answers these questions in his Word, the Bible. We go to the beginning of the Bible and the beginning of life here on earth. In the beginning God creates the heavens and the earth and everything in them. The very best that God creates is a man named Adam and his wife named Eve. God places them in the beautiful Garden of Eden. In that garden are two trees. One tree is the tree of life. This tree gives eternal life to all who eat its fruit. The other tree is the tree of the knowledge of good and evil. God commands Adam and Eve not to eat the fruit found on this tree. He reminds them that if they eat fruit from the tree of the knowledge of good and evil, they will surely die. This is God's command. This is what would happen if Adam and Eve disobey God.

1. The very best that God creates is a man named _____ and his wife named _____.

2. God commands Adam and Eve not to eat the fruit on the tree of the knowledge of _____ and _____.

3. If Adam and Eve eat fruit from the tree of the knowledge of good and evil, they will surely _____.

(Answers to these questions are found on page 25)

Then Satan, or the devil, enters the picture. The devil is an evil angel. When God created our world he also created many angels. Angels are invisible creatures who worship and serve God. But some of the angels, led by the devil, revolted against God, and God threw them out of heaven. The leader of these evil angels was Satan, also called the devil. It is the devil who now comes to Eve in the Garden of Eden. He plants doubt in the heart and mind of Eve. He asks her, "Did God really say that you will die if you eat of the fruit of the tree of the knowledge of good and evil?" The devil also deceives Eve by telling her she would become wise like God if she eats the fruit of the tree. Eve looks at the fruit and it does look good to eat. She eats some of the fruit and gives some to Adam, and he also eats some of the fruit. This is what happened. Adam and Eve disobeyed God. They ate fruit from the tree that God told them they should not eat. They SINNED. (Read Genesis chapter 3).

4. The leader of the evil angels is _____, also called the _____.

5. The devil plants _____ in the heart and mind of Eve.

6. Adam and Eve _____ God.

(Answers to these questions are found on page 25)

The sinfulness of Adam and Eve is passed down to every person in the world. I inherit it from my parents just as I might inherit my parent's physical property. The Bible reminds me, "I know I have been a sinner ever since I was born. I have been a sinner ever since my mother became pregnant with me" (Psalm 51:5). This sin is called inherited sin or original sin. I get it from my sinful parents, and I pass it on to my children.

When God looks at me, he sees not only this inherited sin, but all the sins I commit in my everyday life. God gives me many commands in my life. For example, in Exodus chapter 20 he gives me the Ten Commandments. These commandments remind me that when I steal something from someone else, I sin. When I hurt or hate my friends and neighbors, I sin. When I say bad things about other people, I sin. When I do not obey my parents, I sin. And I could go on to show more examples of how everyone sins against God every day.

The first of God's commandments is the heart of all the other commandments. Whenever I disobey God in any way, I am sinning against the first commandment. In the first commandment I learn: "You shall have no other Gods. What does this mean? We should fear, love and trust in God above all things." This does not mean I must be afraid of God. It means I should respect and honor him. I should love God. I can love God only because he first loved me. I can trust God because he does not lie and he has kept all the promises he made. In other words I should make God most important in all I do and say in my life. He is the true God - Father, Son and Holy Spirit.

7. The sinfulness of Adam and Eve is passed down to _____ person in the world.

8. This sin is called _____ sin or _____ sin.

9. We pass this sin on to our _____.

(Answers to these questions are found on page 25)

The Bible also tells me how inherited sin and the sins I commit every day in my life affect me. God says that the pay I get for sin is death. This death is not just death at the end of my life when my body is put into a grave. It is eternal death in hell. That is what I deserve because of my sins. But even before I die other things happen in my life to remind me that I am a sinner. When I work hard, I get pains in my back and arms and legs. When I don't eat good food or when I eat the wrong food, I get sick and may even need to go to the doctor and use medicine.

While I might have sickness in my body, I also have sickness in my soul. There are people who make my life miserable. They may laugh at me because I believe in Jesus. They may not speak to me or even hurt me because of my faith in Jesus.

And then there are many temptations that try to drag me down. My sinful flesh, the people of this world, and the devil tempt me. They cause me to doubt what God says just as the devil tempted Eve. They may tempt me to see how good other things that I do not have seem to be. Alcohol and drugs that people use look good to me. But when I use them, it harms my body. I become angry with my wife and sin. All these things are the result of my sinful nature and the sins I commit in my life.

10. The pay I get for sin is _____.

11. This death is not just death at the end of my life. It is _____ death in _____.

12. While I might have sickness in my body, I also have sickness in my _____.

13. There are many _____ that come into my life.

14. My sinful _____, the _____ of this world and the _____ tempt me.

(Answers to these questions are found on page 25)

I break God's laws and deserve to die. But as a believer in Jesus I am blessed. Jesus kept God's law perfectly in order to save me from death and in order to show me how to thank God for saving me. The writer to the Hebrews tells me in Hebrews 4:15 that Jesus was "tempted in every way, just as we are. But he did not sin." Jesus was tempted by the devil after Jesus lived without food for 40 days in the wilderness near the city of Jerusalem. The devil tried to plant doubt in Jesus' heart and mind by saying, "If you are the Son of God change these stones into bread." Jesus overcame that temptation by using the Word of God. Then the devil took Jesus to a high place on the temple in the city of Jerusalem. He wanted Jesus to jump down to the ground. This time the devil used Scripture, but he did not quote Scripture correctly and tried to deceive Jesus. Jesus once again used Scripture, answering the devil that he should not tempt God. Finally, the devil took Jesus to a very high mountain. He asked Jesus to bow down and worship him, and he would give Jesus all he could see. But once again Jesus used the Word of God and said, "It is written. Worship the Lord your God. He is the only one you should serve" (Matthew 4:10).

15. Jesus kept God's law _____.

16. The writer to the Hebrews tells us that Jesus was "tempted in every way, just as we are. But he did _____ sin."

17. Jesus was tempted by the devil three times. Jesus overcame these temptations by using the _____ of God.

(Answers to these questions are found on page 25)

Jesus is the answer to overcoming sin in my life. He used God's Word when he was tempted by the devil. I can use God's Word too. I can pray to Jesus to lead me through God's Word to overcome the devil in my life. We will learn more about this in Chapter Four when we talk about living a Christian life.

- The Bible tells me I am a sinner from the time I was born.
- The Bible tells me the pay I receive because of my sins is death.
- The Bible tells me Jesus is without sin because he is the Son of God.
- The Bible tells me Jesus overcame the temptations of the devil by using the Word of God.

- Now I can use God's Word to overcome temptation and sin in my life.
- My remedy for sin is found in the Bible.

**Chief of sinners though I be,
Jesus shed his blood for me,
Died that I might live on high,
Lived that I might never die.
As the branch is to the vine,
I am his and he is mine. (CW 385)**

Review of Chapter Two

God's Word tells me how sin came into our world. God creates Adam and Eve as our first parents and tells them not to eat of the tree of the knowledge of good and evil. Satan, or the devil, is an angel that rebelled against God and was thrown out of heaven. The devil tempts Eve to eat of the tree that God told her not to eat. The devil causes Eve to doubt God's Word.

She sees the fruit on the tree is good. She eats it and gives some to Adam to eat. They disobey

God. They sin. This sin is called inherited sin or original sin. Every person born in the world from the time of Adam and Eve has this inherited sin. I also have other sins I commit each day of my life. When I steal, hate someone or hurt them, when I say bad things about someone, I sin. I sin against the very first commandment when I do not put God first in my life. I should honor God, love him and trust him. I don't always do that. I sin. My own sinful flesh, the people of the world and the devil – all three tempt me to sin.

But I am blessed. God's Word teaches me that Jesus is without sin. He kept the law of God perfectly. He was tempted by the devil, but he overcame the temptations of the devil by using God's Word. I too can use God's Word to overcome temptations in my life. I learn how to do this from the Bible.

Answers to the questions in Chapter Two:
1. Adam, Eve; 2. good, evil; 3. die; 4. Satan, devil; 5. doubt; 6. disobeyed; 7. every; 8. inherited, original; 9. children; 10. death; 11. eternal, hell; 12. soul; 13. temptations; 14. flesh, people, devil; 15. perfectly; 16. not; 17. Word.

Chapter Two Test

1. God commands Adam and Eve not to eat the fruit on the tree of the knowledge of _____ and _____.

2. If Adam and Eve eat of the fruit of the tree of the knowledge of good and evil they would surely _____.

3. The leader of the evil angels is _____ also called the _____.

4. Adam and Eve _____ God.

5. The sinfulness of Adam and Eve is passed down to _____ person in the world.

6. This sin is called _____ sin, or _____ sin.

7. The pay I get for sin is _____.

8. My sinful _____, the _____ of this world and the _____ tempt me.

9. Jesus kept God's law _____.

10. Jesus was tempted by the devil three times. Jesus overcame these temptations by using the _____ of God.

(Answers to these questions is found on page 97)

Learn how people in the Bible were tempted to sin:

Genesis 39:1-20 - Joseph is tempted to commit adultery.

1 Kings 21:1-29 - King Ahab has an evil desire for Naboth's vineyard.

Ephesians 6:10-18 - I can overcome the devil by using God's Word.

Jesus speaks to Nicodemus - John 3:1-16

Chapter Three

God's Word shows me God's love

I want to begin this chapter about how God's Word shows me God's love by telling you about a man by the name of Myimba. Myimba was a farmer in Central Africa. He was a very good farmer. He was so good that the government awarded him a new plow. Myimba came to worship services every week. Worship was held near the Shibyungi agricultural station in what is now the country of Zambia in Africa. Each week I also had a Bible study class on Wednesday afternoon. Myimba attended faithfully. We were studying the book of Galatians in the New Testament. As we were studying this book one afternoon Myimba suddenly stood up with a smile on his face that stretched from ear to ear. He said, "For the first time in my life I know and am certain that I am not saved by the good works or deeds that I do, but I am saved by faith in Jesus Christ, my Savior." Myimba was a happy man. Like Myimba, my heart is filled with joy to know that I am not saved by my own good works. I too am blessed because God in his love shows me in his Word that I am saved through what Jesus did for me. Learn what God's Word says:

> * God promises to send a Savior, and he did send a Savior, and

> * God saves me by grace through faith in that Savior.

God does love me. God promised to send a Savior to our first parents, Adam and Eve, after they fell into sin by eating of the forbidden fruit on the tree of the knowledge of good and evil in the Garden of Eden. God promised them that a child born in the future would defeat the devil and end the power that death has over everyone. Many years later the prophet Isaiah tells us, "The Lord himself will give you a miraculous sign. The virgin is going to have a baby. She will give birth to a son. And he will be called Immanuel" (Isaiah 7:14). Immanuel means

God with us. Jesus is that baby. He is God with us. Later another prophet named Micah tells us this baby will be born in the village of Bethlehem. "The Lord says, Bethlehem, you might not be an important town in the nation of Judah. But out of you will come a ruler over Israel for me" (Micah 5:2). Then hundreds of years later God keeps his promise. When the proper time comes he sends his only Son, Jesus, born of the virgin Mary in the town of Bethlehem in the country of Judea. Read Galatians chapter 4 verses 4 through 7. This is good news. Also, read Luke chapter 2 verses 1 through 20. God promises to send a Savior. He keeps that promise when Jesus is born to be my Savior. Now I, as a child of God, can call God my Father.

1. God promises to send a _____ to our first parents _____ and _____.

2. The _____ is going to have a baby.

3. He will be called Immanuel. Immanuel means _____ _____ _____.

4. The prophet Micah tells us this baby will be born in the town of _____.

5. God sends his only Son, Jesus, born of the virgin _____ in the town of _____.

6. God keeps his promise when Jesus is born to be my _____.

7. Now I, as a child of God, can call God my _____.

(Answers to these questions are found on page 39)

Jesus humbled himself and was born as a human being in order to live under God's law. At the same time, as true God, Jesus kept the law for me perfectly. God demands that I live a perfect life. I cannot keep God's law perfectly. If I sin in one part of the law, God's Word tells me I sin against all of God's law. Look at this example: A chain reaches from one post to another post. It doesn't make any difference which link in the chain breaks. It can be a link near the post. It can be one halfway to the next post. But if a link in the chain breaks, it will not reach from one post to the other. The same is true of God's law. If we break only one of the commandments we cannot reach heaven from earth by keeping God's law.

Jesus shows me God's love by keeping all of God's law for me. The Bible tells me Jesus, as a child, obeyed his parents. Read Luke chapter 2 verses 41 through 52. God's Word tells me that Jesus did not sin. The apostle Peter writes, "He (Jesus) didn't commit any sin. No lies ever came out of his mouth" (1 Peter 2:22). I lie because I am a sinful human being but Jesus did not lie and kept the law for me perfectly.

8. We cannot keep God's law _____.

9. Jesus shows us God's _____ for me by keeping all of God's _____ for us.

10. God's Word tells us that Jesus did not _____.

(Answers to these questions are found on page 39)

God's love for me is shown in Jesus being punished for my sins. When I break God's law, I deserve to die. Jesus took my place and died on the cross. Jesus was innocent but was punished for me. When Jesus died on the cross he cried out, "It is finished." By those words Jesus meant he finished the work of saving me. God is satisfied with what Jesus did for me. On the third day after Jesus died on the cross, he rose from death. Read Matthew chapter 28 verses 1 through 7. This shows that God was satisfied. Then he exalted

Jesus to the highest heaven, "He (Jesus) obeyed God completely, even though it led to his death. In fact, he died on a cross. So God lifted him up to the highest place. He gave him the name that is above every name. When the name of Jesus is spoken, every knee will bow to worship him. Every knee in heaven and on earth and under the earth will bow to worship him. Everyone's mouth will say that Jesus Christ is Lord. And God the Father will receive glory" (Philippians 2:8-11). I am blessed. God's Word assures me that God the Father loves me. He sent Jesus to keep God's law for me. Jesus bore the punishment for my sins. I am now forgiven and have the hope of going to heaven. When I die I will be with Jesus forever.

11. God's love for me is shown by Jesus being _____ for my sins.

12. Jesus took my place and died on the _____.

13. After Jesus died on the cross he _____ from _____.

14. Every knee will bow to _____ him (Jesus).

(Answers for these questions are found on page 39)

All this happens because of God's undeserved love. We call this undeserved love God's grace. I am saved by God's grace. The apostle Paul writes, "God's grace has saved you [through] faith in Christ. Your salvation does not come from anything you do. It is God's gift. It is not based on anything you have done. No one can brag about earning it" (Ephesians 2:8-9). Remember what Myimba, the African farmer, said? He was happy he learned he is not saved by his own works, but that he is saved by God's grace, the love he did not deserve. I am also saved by God's grace.

God even gives me faith to believe in Jesus, my Savior. "Faith comes from hearing the message. And the message that is heard is the word of Christ" (Romans 10:17). I am blessed through God's Word. Because of God's love for me, I am saved by God's grace through faith. Jesus is the only way to go to heaven. He tells us, "I am the way and the truth and the life. No one comes to the Father except through me" (John 14:6). The apostle Peter tells me the same thing. "You cannot be saved by believing in anyone else. God has given us no other name under heaven that will save us" (Acts 4:12). Jesus is my only Savior. I do not deserve God's blessing, but he gives it to me without any cost to me. It cost Jesus much.

Therefore, I will raise my voice in praise to God. I will tell my friends and neighbors about God's great love that I receive through Jesus, my Savior. I will praise God with a Christian life. The next chapter in this book will tell how God blesses me with a Christian life while I live on earth.

15. God's undeserved love is called _____.

16. I am _____ by God's grace.

17. God even gives me _____ to believe in Jesus, my Savior.

(Answers to these questions are found on page 39)

I am blessed because God's Word shows me God's love.

- The Bible tells me I am a sinner.
- The Bible tells me Jesus lived a perfect life and did not sin.
- The Bible tells me I deserve to die eternally because of my sin.
- The Bible tells me Jesus died on the cross and bore the punishment for my sins.
- The Bible tells me God's grace, his undeserved love, saves me.

- The Bible tells me God gives me faith through his Word to believe in Jesus.
- I am blessed through God's Word.
- I will worship and praise Jesus for all he has done for me.

Abide, O dearest Jesus,
among us with your grace
That Satan may not harm us
nor we to sin give place.

Abide, O dear Redeemer,
among us with your Word
And thus now, and hereafter
true peace and joy afford. (CW 333)

Review of Chapter Three

I am blessed through God's Word, the Bible. I learn that I am a sinner and deserve to be punished because of my sins. However, God loves me and sent Jesus to be my Savior. God promised to send a Savior, and he keeps his promises. Jesus was born of the virgin Mary in the village of Bethlehem.

Jesus came to do for me what I cannot do. He kept God's law perfectly for me. Only the Son of God can do that. Jesus also was punished for my sins. He died on a cross. When he cried out, "It is finished," Jesus finished the work of saving me and everyone who lives on earth. God was satisfied that Jesus kept the law and suffered for everyone's sins. God raised Jesus from the dead and gave him great glory in heaven

God loves me. I do not deserve God's love. That undeserved love is called grace. I am saved by God's grace through faith in Jesus. Even my faith is a gift of God. Therefore, I cannot brag that I can save myself. Jesus is the only way to be right with God. God does everything for me. As a result, I now praise God and worship him with all my heart.

I am blessed through God's Word because the Bible tells me that I am saved and all my sins are forgiven because of what Jesus did for me.

Answers to the questions in Chapter Three:
1. Savior, Adam, Eve; 2. virgin; 3. God with us; 4. Bethlehem;
5. Mary, Bethlehem; 6. Savior; 7. Father; 8. perfectly; 9. love, law;
10. sin; 11. punished; 12. cross; 13. rose, death; 14. worship;
15. grace; 16. saved; 17. faith.

Chapter Three Test

1. God promised to send a _____ to our first parents _____ and _____.

2. God sent his only Son, Jesus, born of the virgin _____ in the town of _____.

3. Jesus shows us God's _____ for us by keeping all of God's _____ for us.

4. God's Word tells us that Jesus did not _____.

5. Jesus took our place and died on the _____.

6. God's undeserved love is called _____.

7. I am _____ by God's grace.

8. God even gives me _____ to believe in Jesus, my Savior.

(Answers to these questions are found on page 97)

Learn how God saves people by his grace through faith:

John 21:15-19 - Jesus forgives Peter even though Peter sinned against Jesus.

John 20:24-29 -The apostle Thomas believes that Jesus is his Lord and God.

John 20:30,31 - Through God's Word I also believe that Jesus is my Savior.

*The Good Samaritan helps the man who is hurt -
Luke 10:25-35*

Chapter Four

God's Word blesses me in my life on earth

As a believing child of God I am blessed in many ways. One of the ways God blesses me is to guide me by his Word in my everyday life.

It makes a great difference if a person believes what God says or if someone does not believe God.

An unbeliever does not follow God's Word and in many cases falls into great sin. Such sins may include drunkenness, abuse of a wife or children, stealing things that do not belong to him or her, failure to discipline sons or daughters. The life of an unbeliever can be a very unhappy life.

A believer, who is blessed with God's Word, will follow that Word and be a loving husband and father. He works hard to supply food, clothing and a home for his family. He worships God faithfully and serves God as he is able with joy. I am blessed, I had Christian parents. Remembering Christian parents is also a blessing. "To remember those who do right is a blessing" (Proverbs 10:7).

What a blessing it is to be a God-pleasing Christian.

As God blesses me, I want to be a blessing to others. Therefore, this chapter teaches:

> * God's Word guides me in my Christian life, and
>
> * God's Word fills my life with joy and peace.

In thanksgiving to my loving God I want to live my life in praise to my Lord and Savior Jesus Christ for all he has done for me. I want to live a Christian life, but not to gain salvation by my good works. Jesus lived and died for me to save me. My Christian life is lived in thanks to God for my salvation. I am blessed. God's Word guides me in my life. The Bible shows me how to live with love for my family, my church, my government and my neighbors.

A loving family is a blessing from God. When God created Adam and Eve, he made Eve as Adam's helper. "The man said, her bones have come from my bones. Her body has come from my body. She will be called 'woman' because she was taken out of a man. That is why a man will leave his father and mother and be joined to his wife. The two of them will become one flesh" (Genesis 2:23,24). God guides me by telling me that a true God-pleasing marriage is one between a man and a woman. God's Word also tells me how a husband and wife are to care for each other. "Husbands, love your wives. Love them just as Christ loved the church. He gave himself for her" (Ephesians 5:25). Here Jesus is an example for husbands. God's Word guides me to show love, sacrificial love, toward my wife. And he guides wives also. "Wives follow the lead of your husbands as you follow the lead of the Lord. The husband is the head of the wife, just as Christ is the head of the church…. He is its Savior." (Ephesians 5:23). As the church honors Christ, the wife is to honor and respect her husband.

1. My Christian life is lived in _____ to God for my _____.

2. A loving family is a _____ from God.

3. A true God-pleasing marriage is one between a _____ and a _____.

4. God's Word guides me to show _____, sacrificial _____, toward my wife.

5. As the church honors Christ, the wife is to _____ and _____ her husband.

(Answers for these questions are found on page 58)

In our families there is to be a loving relationship not only between the husband and the wife, but also between parents and children. God's Word is our guide. It reminds me that children are a blessing from the Lord. As a parent, I should take good care of my children. The apostle Paul writes, "Everyone [and this includes parents] should take care of his own family. If he doesn't, he has left the faith. He is worse than someone who doesn't believe" (1Timothy 5:8). In fact, he tells parents, and especially "Fathers, don't make your children angry. Instead train them and teach them the ways of the Lord as you raise them" (Ephesians 6:4). I have a responsibility to see that my children are taught God's Word so that it will be a guide in their lives. Children also have a responsibility in the family. "Children, obey your parents as believers in the Lord. Obey them because it's the right thing to do" (Ephesians 6:1). Children love and respect their parents by doing what they are told to do. God promises a long life on earth to children who obey their parents. "Listen to your father, who gave you life. Don't hate your mother when she is old." (Proverbs 23:22).

God's Word is my guide in my family life. Unfortunately, I do not always love my wife as I should. My children do not always honor me as their father. At those times I can turn to God's Word and seek forgiveness as well as show forgiveness that my Savior has won for me. I am blessed. God's Word guides me in my family life and gives me forgiveness. His word gives me faith in what Jesus has done for me.

6. God's Word reminds me that children are a _____ from the Lord.

7. I have a responsibility to see that my children are taught _____ _____.

8. A child shows honor and _____ to his or her parents by doing what they are told to do.

(Answers to these questions are found on page 58)

My love for the church of Jesus Christ and my fellow Christians is very important to me. Through the power of the Holy Spirit, I have become a member of God's church along with many other believers. The Holy Spirit has done this through the power of the gospel in God's Word and the sacraments of Holy Baptism and Holy Communion.

As a believer I want to worship the Lord. Jesus loved me so much by keeping the law for me and bearing the punishment for my sins. I am a forgiven child of God. In response to all Jesus has done for me, I love him and want to praise him. I can do this through my prayer life and my worship life.

Jesus asks me to pray to him. He says, "My Father will give you anything you ask for in my name" (John 16:23). But sometimes it seems I do not receive what I ask for. Then I need to remember that God may answer my prayer by giving me exactly what I want, or he may say "wait," or he may even say "take this instead" to my prayer. For example, if a small child wants a sharp knife, will a mother give that knife to the child? No! Why? Because the mother knows the knife will harm the child. The same thing is true with God. If he sees that what I ask for will harm me, he will answer my prayer in a better way instead. Therefore, I will continue to ask God for what I need in my life knowing that God is a loving Father, and I am his dear child. Jesus, in a sermon, tells us, "Even though you are evil, you know how to give good gifts to your children. How much more will your Father who is in heaven give good gifts to those who ask him?" (Matthew 7:11). I will not only ask for things from God, but I will continue to thank and praise him for all he does for me.

While I can and should pray to God daily, I also have the opportunity to worship him when I go to church. In the church worship service, I confess my sins and receive the announcement of my forgiveness. I also hear God's Word read and then also explained in a sermon. I join other Christians in praying to God, and I love singing hymns of praise. God reminds me in his Ten Commandments that I should "Remember the Sabbath day (or day of rest) by keeping it holy." I should gladly hear and learn God's Word. In answer to God's desire to bless my life, I answer with the Psalm writer and say, "I was very glad when they said to me, 'Let us go up to the house of the Lord'" (Psalm 122:1). What a joy it is for me to worship the Lord my God. I am blessed. I can joyfully worship the Lord together with other believers.

As a child of God I also want to support the work of my church. In thankfulness for God's love and all he has done for me, I will give of my time, my spiritual gifts, and even of my money to support the work of God's church. The apostle Paul writes, "You should each give what you have decided in your heart to give. You shouldn't give if you don't want to. You shouldn't give because you are forced to. God loves a cheerful giver" (2 Corinthians 9:7). Out of love for my Savior, I will then support the work of God's church cheerfully and to the best of my ability to do so.

9. As a believer I want to _____ the Lord.

10. In response to all Jesus has done for me, I want to _____ him.

11. Jesus asks me to _____ to him.

12. I will not only _____ for things from God, but I will continue to _____ and _____ him for all he does for me.

13. God reminds me in his Ten Commandments that I should "Remember the Sabbath day or day of rest by keeping it _____."

14. I should _____ hear and learn God's Word.

15. Out of love for my Savior, I will then _____ the work of God's church.

(Answers to these questions are found on page 58)

When I am blessed through God's Word, I not only love my family and other believers in the church, but I also show love to God and to other people by respecting the government God has placed over me. Just as God established the church, he also established the government to rule over me. It does not matter what kind of government it is. If it is a democracy, a kingdom or a dictatorship, God established it. The apostle Paul tells us, "All of you must be willing to obey completely those who rule over you. There are no authorities except the ones God has chosen. Those who now rule have been chosen by God" (Romans 13:1). God's Word guides us in this matter. The apostle Peter also tells us, "Follow the lead of every human authority. Do it because the Lord wants you to. Obey the king. He is the highest authority. Obey the governors" (1 Peter 2:13,14). As a citizen in my country, I obey the government. If I do what is good, I do not need to be afraid because I will be praised for doing good. However, if I break the laws of my country, then the government has the right and duty to punish me.

I should support the government. I can do this by paying taxes. Jesus himself reminds us of this. When some of Jesus' enemies wanted to catch him in saying something wrong, they asked him, "Tell us then, what do you think? Is it right to pay taxes to Caesar or not? But Jesus knew their evil plans... Then he said to them, 'Give to Caesar what belongs to Caesar. And give to God what belongs to God'" (Matthew 22:17,21).

I also should pray for my government and its officials. The apostle Paul tells Timothy and me, "First, I want all of you to pray for everyone. Ask God to bless them. Give thanks for them. Pray for kings. Pray for all who are in authority. Pray that we will live peaceful and quiet lives. And pray that we will be godly and holy" (1 Timothy 2:1,2). What a blessing to be guided by God's Word to pray for those over me in the government so I can live a peaceful and quiet life. As a follower of Jesus, I want to be guided by God's Word. I want to have a happy and quiet life in my home and in my village and in my country.

16. Just as God established the church, he has also established the _____ to rule over us.

17. As a citizen in my country I should _____ the government.

18. I can support the government by paying _____.

19. I should _____ for my government and its officials so I can live a _____ and _____ life.

(Answers to these questions are found on page 58)

My neighbor is sick. He can't go out to work in his fields. He cannot take care of his animals. What should I do? I am blessed. God's Word guides me so I know what to do. "So when we can do good to everyone, let us do it. Let us make a special point of doing good to those who belong to the family of believers" (Galatians 6:10). What should I do when someone needs help? I should help him or her. Perhaps I can do some of his work so he does not worry. Perhaps I can give him or her food or money so they can care for the needs of their family. I should not become tired of doing good to others.

Indeed, I am blessed through God's Word. The Holy Spirit, using God's Word, guides my love for my family, my church, my government and also my neighbor. God guides me in my Christian life so I can be a blessing to other people, especially to God's family.

Showing love brings joy to my life. Again and again God's Word reminds us to be happy, to be joyful, and to rejoice. "When you hope, be joyful. When you suffer, be patient. When you pray, be faithful. Share with God's people who are in need. Welcome others into your home. Be joyful with those who are joyful" (Romans 12:12,15).

Love brings peace into my life. Through faith in Jesus, I am at peace with God. I do not need to be afraid of God because he has forgiven me. Living a Christian, loving life I am also at peace with my fellow man. There is peace in my family, in my church, in the government and with my neighbors.

20. What should I do when someone needs help? I should _____ him.

21. I can be a _____ to other people, especially to God's family.

22. Through faith in Jesus, I am at _____ with God.

23. Living a Christian, loving life I am also at _____ with my fellow man.

(Answers to these questions are found on page 58)

I am blessed through God's Word. His Word guides me in my life on earth and leads me to eternal life in heaven with Jesus.

- God's Word guides me in showing love to my wife or husband.
- God's Word guides me in showing love to my children and guides them to respect me.
- God's Word guides me to pray for others, not just for myself.
- God's Word guides me to worship and praise God because of all he has done for me.
- God's Word guides me to show honor and respect for all who rule over me.

- God's Word guides me to help my neighbor in whatever way needed by my neighbor.
- God's Word guides me to live in peace with God and my fellow man.

**What a friend we have in Jesus,
all our sins and griefs to bear.
What a privilege to carry
everything to God in prayer!
Oh, what peace we often forfeit,
Oh, what needless pain we bear.
All because we do not carry
everything to God in prayer! (CW 411)**

Review of Chapter Four

God's Word serves as a guide to show me how I should live as a Christian. Jesus saves me, but it is the Holy Spirit who guides me to show love to members of my family and my church and to those over me in the government as well as those who are my neighbors.

In a Christian family, husbands should love their wives and wives should honor and respect their husbands who are the head of the family. Children are to obey their parents and parents, in love, are to teach God's Word to their children.

In my church I learn to pray to Jesus at all times and to worship him by confessing my sins, receiving his forgiveness, listening to God's Word read and explained, as well as by singing songs of praise to God for all the blessings he gives to me. I will support my church in whatever way I can.

In my life as a citizen of my country, I will respect those over me in the government, pray for them, and support my government by paying my taxes. When I respect the government and obey its laws, I will be blessed.

I should be a neighbor to those around me in my life. When I see that they have problems because they are sick or need help, I will show love to them and help them.

By doing God's will in my Christian life, I find joy and happiness. I am at peace with God and all who live near me and who are over me and need my help. I am blessed through God's Word.

Answers to the questions in Chapter Four:
1. thanks, salvation; 2. blessing; 3. man, woman; 4. love, love;
5. honor, respect; 6. blessing; 7. God's Word; 8. respect;
9. worship; 10. praise; 11. pray; 12. ask, thank, praise; 13. holy;
14. gladly; 15. support; 16. government; 17. obey; 18. taxes;
19. pray, peaceful, quiet; 20. help; 21. blessing; 22. peace;
23. peace.

Chapter Four Test

1. A loving family is a _____ from God.

2. A true God-pleasing marriage is one between a _____ and _____.

3. I have a responsibility to see that my children are taught _____ _____.

4. I will not only _____ for things from God, but will continue to _____ and _____ him for all he does for me.

5. God reminds me in his Ten Commandments that I should "Remember the Sabbath day or day of rest by keeping it _____."

6. I should _____ hear and learn God's Word.

7. As a citizen of my country I should _____ the government.

8. I can support the government by paying _____.

9. What should I do when someone needs help? I should _____ him.

10. Through faith in Jesus, I am at _____ with God.

11. Living a Christian, loving life I am also at _____ with my fellow man.

(Answers to these questions can be found on page 97)

Study how God's Word guides me to live a Christian life:

Ephesians 5:22-6:4 - The apostle Paul teaches about family relationships.

Luke 2:41-52 - Jesus studies God's Word and obeys his parents.

Romans 13:1-7 - My government is to be respected.

Luke 10:25-37 - I should help those who need my help.

Jesus comforts Martha at Lazarus' grave - John 11:17-44

Chapter Five

God's Word guides and helps me during days of suffering

Let me tell you about a Lutheran pastor who lived many years ago in the country of Germany. His name is Paul Gerhardt. Throughout his ministry he faced many trials and much suffering. His hometown was completely destroyed during war. Four of his five children died in the first year of their lives. His wife also died. And yet, he did not get angry with God. Through God's Word, he struggled to overcome all these sufferings and he became a great hymn writer. Many of his beautiful hymns praise God during his sufferings such as, "I will sing my Maker's praises" or "Why should cross and trial grieve me?"

In our lives we also face many sufferings such as lack of food for our families and ourselves, death of loved ones and sickness that we suffer. As a young boy I grew up at a time when many people did not have work or the money to buy food. I remember that for at least one week each month, we had very little to eat. Later in life, my wife faced cancer operations, and now I am also very sick. Recently our only son died unexpectedly at a young age. But you know, it is God and his Word that are with me during all of these sufferings. He guides me and promises to help me. Jesus tells his disciples, "You can be sure that I am always with you, to the very end" (Matthew 28:20).

1. In our lives we face many _____.

2. Write down some of the sufferings you have in your life.
   _____
   _____

3. It is God and his _____ that are with us during all our sufferings.

4. God guides us and promises to _____ us.

(Answers to these questions can be found on page 73)

Therefore, in this lesson we learn:

* Jesus used his Word to guide people when suffering came into their lives, and

* Jesus helps us to overcome the sufferings we experience in our lives.

First of all, I want you to think about a man named Job, who lives during the Old Testament. He is a very rich man with huge flocks of sheep, herds of camels, donkeys, and many servants, as well as ten sons and daughters. One day he learns that his enemies took away his sheep, donkeys, and camels. They also killed most of Job's servants. Then he receives a report that a strong wind destroyed the house in which his children are enjoying a meal. All of his children are killed. Finally, Job is covered with painful sores from the bottom of his feet to the top of his head. Truly, Job's life is filled with much suffering. Job's wife tells him to curse God and die. Some friends want to know what sin Job did to deserve such great suffering. But Job does not curse God. The Bible tells us, "In spite of everything Job didn't sin by blaming God for doing anything wrong" (Job 1:22). In all of his suffering, the Lord speaks to Job. As a result of God's guiding hand, Job is able to confess, "I know that my Redeemer lives. In the end he will stand on the earth. After my skin has been destroyed, in my body I'll still see God. I myself will see him with my own eyes. I'll see him and he won't be a stranger to me. How my heart longs for that day" (Job 19:25-27). Job's faith remains strong and he looks forward to the goal ahead of every believer – seeing God face to face in heaven. Even though Job experiences much suffering in his life, he looks to God to help him and looks forward to living in heaven. Later in Job's life on earth, God restores his health and blesses him with ten more children and large flocks of sheep and herds of camels, donkeys and oxen.

5. Job lived during the _____ _____.

6. Job was a very _____ man.

7. In all of his suffering the _____ speaks to Job.

8. Job looks forward to living in _____.

(Answers to these questions can be found on page 73)

Another person who followed God's guidance was the apostle Paul. He had a "thorn in the flesh," "a pain in my body" (2 Corinthians 12:7). We do not know what Paul's painful condition was. Some think his hands were crippled from making tents out of heavy cloth. Others think he could not see well. Whatever Paul's problem was, he prayed to God to take it away. However, God answered him saying, "My grace is all you need. My power is strongest when you are weak" (2 Corinthians 12:9). God did not take away Paul's suffering. However, God gave him the power to bear his suffering.

9. Paul _____ to God to take away his "pain in his body."

10. God did _____ take away Paul's suffering.

11. God gave Paul the _____ to bear his suffering.

(Answers to these questions can be found on page 73)

What God did for Job and Paul, he also promises to do for me. For the past months I have had great pain. I cannot walk as I should. Besides having bad headaches, I also am losing a lot of weight. I have gone to many doctors, but a solution to my suffering has not been found. Yet, I am certain that Jesus is with me in my suffering. He promises, as he did to Joshua, "The Lord… will be with you. He will never leave you. He'll never desert you. So don't be afraid. Don't lose hope" (Deuteronomy 31:8). God promises to guide and help me when I am suffering. I am blessed. God hears my prayers. He gives me the strength to face pain and suffering just as he did for Jesus.

Sometimes we suffer because we are Christians. People may laugh when we study God's Word or when we worship him. People may not listen to us when we want to speak to them about Jesus. I remember one day in the country of Bulgaria. I was handing out Christian literature as people came into the market. Some of the Christian literature was thrown on the ground. One man came up to me and told me to go home, pointing to me and hitting me on my chest. It hurt my heart to know that people did not want to learn about Jesus. I may be laughed at, ignored or even hurt, but I need to remember what God's Word tells me, "A servant is not better than his master" (Matthew 10:24). If people laughed at Jesus and would not listen to him, as a Christian, I can expect to suffer when I confess Jesus. The apostle Peter tells us in his letter in the Bible, "Who is going to hurt you if you really want to do good? But suppose you suffer for doing what is right. Then you will be blessed" (1 Peter 3:13,14). Then Peter reminds us how, even in the midst of suffering, we should continue to tell others about Jesus, "But make sure in your hearts that Christ is Lord. Always be ready to give an answer to anyone who asks you about the hope you have. Be ready to give the reason for it. But do it gently and with respect" (1 Peter 3:15).

12. What God did for Job and Paul, he promises to do for _____.

13. God promises to guide and _____ us when we are suffering.

14. God gives me the strength to face pain and suffering just as he did for _____.

(Answers to these questions can be found on page 73)

Remember how Jesus prays to God in the Garden of Gethsemane on the night he was betrayed by Judas? He is alone because his disciples, Peter, James and John fall asleep. He prays so hard that his sweat falls like great drops of blood. He asks that the cup of his suffering might pass from him. He says, "My Father, if it is possible, take this cup of suffering away from me, but let what you want be done, not what I want" (Matthew 26:39). God does not take away that suffering. Jesus suffers and dies for each one of us. By his suffering and death on the cross, he pays for all of my sins so I may be forgiven and live with him in heaven. Suffering, whatever form it takes, can turn out to be a blessing for me and for you.

15. Jesus asks that the cup of his _____ might pass from him.

16. God does _____ take away Jesus' suffering.

17. By his suffering and death on the cross Jesus pays for all of our _____ so we may be _____ and live with him in _____.

(Answers to these questions can be found on page 73)

I am blessed through God's Word.

- I am certain God will guide me and protect me.
- I can pray to God for help when I face suffering.
- I leave it in God's hands to remove my suffering.
- I praise and thank God for his help.
- I remember Jesus' suffering for me.

- I look for the day when I will be with Jesus in heaven and all the sufferings of this present life will be gone.

Be still my soul, the Lord is on your side;
Bear patiently the cross of grief or pain;
Leave to your God to order and provide;
In every change, he faithful will remain.
Be still my soul,
your best, your heavenly friend
Through thorny ways
leads to a joyful end. (CW 415)

Review of Chapter Four

In our lives we experience many sufferings. Lack of food, sickness, and death may be a part of our lives. It is God who guides and protects us when we face suffering. God did that for a man named Job in Old Testament times. Job was a rich man, but in a short time his large flocks of sheep and herds of camels and donkeys were taken away from him and his ten children died when a wind destroyed the house in which they were gathered. Job was covered with sores head to toe. Job did not curse God. He remained faithful to God in spite of all his suffering. He looked forward to the time when he would see God face to face.

The apostle Paul also experienced much pain. God did not take the pain away, but gave him the strength to bear the pain. In the same way, God guides me when I suffer. He helps me and takes away the sufferings, or he gives me the strength to endure the sufferings. God leads me through the sufferings of this world to the peace and joy of heaven.

I not only experience physical sufferings, but also spiritual sufferings when people laugh at me because I am a believer or they will not listen to me when I want to tell them about Jesus. Then I can remember that they did that to Jesus, my master, and I can expect they will do the same to me.

Jesus also suffered for us. He prayed to his Father in heaven in the Garden of Gethsemane. His sweat was like great drops of blood. But he left it in God's hands if he must suffer. He said, "Not what I want, but what you want." In the same way I, as a believer, leave it in God's hands to guide and help me as he wills.

Answers to the questions in Chapter Five:
1. sufferings; 2. various answers can be given; 3. Word; 4. help; 5. Old Testament; 6. rich; 7. Lord; 8. heaven; 9. prayed; 10. not; 11. power; 12. us; 13. help; 14. Jesus; 15. suffering; 16. not; 17. sins, forgiven, heaven.

Chapter Five Test

1. In our lives we face many _____.

2. Write down some of the sufferings you have in your life.
   _____
   _____
   _____

3. God guides us and promises to _____ us.

4. Job lived during the _____ _____.

5. Job looked forward to living in _____.

6. Paul _____ to God to take away his "pain in his body."

7. God did _____ take away Paul's suffering.

8. God gave to Paul the _____ to bear his suffering.

9. What God did for Job and Paul, he promises to do for _____.

10. By his suffering and death on the cross Jesus paid for all of our _____ so we may be _____ and live with him in _____.

(Answers to these questions are found on page 97)

Study how God's Word guides and helps us during times of suffering:

Luke 7:11–17 – Jesus helps the widow whose son he raises from the dead.

Mark 2:1–12 – Jesus heals a man who could not walk.

Luke 17:11–19 – Jesus heals ten men.

Matthew 14:13–21 – Jesus feeds over five thousand people.

The glorified Jesus separates the believers from the unbelievers - Matthew 25:31-46

Chapter Six

God's Word leads me to eternal life in heaven

What is heaven going to be like? Some people have different ideas of what living in heaven will be like. There was a young woman who was very sick. She had a serious illness and knew she would die soon. She told me that she thought that in heaven she would see many beautiful flowers. You see, she lived out in the countryside and had many flowers around her home. I don't know if there will be a lot of flowers in heaven, but I do know much about heaven. I am blessed because God's Word tells me about heaven.

After a Christian life here on earth a believer will experience everlasting life in heaven. In this chapter God's Word tells us:

> * Why I will go to heaven,
>
> * What heaven is like, and
>
> * How I want to serve God now and in heaven.

The Bible tells me that God raised Jesus from death on the third day after Jesus died on the cross. We call that day Easter. After his rising from the dead, Jesus remained on earth for 40 days. He appeared to his disciples and many other people to show that he was indeed alive. Then he returned to heaven. Jesus told his disciples, "You will be my witnesses from one end of the earth to the other (Acts 1:8). After Jesus said this, he was taken up to heaven. They (the disciples) watched until a cloud hid him from their sight. While he was going up, they kept looking at the sky. Suddenly two men (angels) dressed in white clothing stood beside them. 'Men of Galilee,' they said, 'why do you stand looking at the sky? Jesus has been taken away from you into heaven. But he will come back in the same way you saw him go'" (Acts 1:8-11).

Yes, I know that Jesus lives and he assures me that because he lives, I will live also and be with him in heaven. He has promised this to me.

At the end of my life on earth, I will die. My body will be laid into a grave. But my soul lives because I believe in Jesus as my Savior, and my soul goes to heaven to be with Jesus. On the Last Day, Jesus will come again and take my body AND my soul to be with him in heaven. "We know that God raised the Lord Jesus from the dead. And he will also raise us up with Jesus. He will bring us with you to God in heaven" (2 Corinthians 4:14). I can be certain that I will see Jesus in heaven. In the last chapter we learned of a man named Job who believed he would see Jesus and said, "I know that my Redeemer lives. In the end he will stand on the earth. After my skin has been destroyed, in my body I'll still see God. I myself will see him with my own eyes. I'll see him, and he won't be a stranger to me. How my heart longs for that day" (Job 19:25-27). Like Job, I am certain that I will see Jesus in heaven. I can be certain of this because of God's love for me. "We owe it all to Christ who has loved us. I am absolutely sure that not even death or life can separate us from God's love. Not even angels or demons, the present or the future, or any powers can do that. Not even the highest places or the lowest, or anything else in all creation can do that. Nothing at all can ever separate us from God's love because of what Christ Jesus our Lord has done" (Romans 8:37-39). Yes! Yes! Yes! I am certain of my salvation because of what Christ has done for me. I will be in heaven with him.

1. God raised Jesus on the third day after Jesus died. We call this day _____.

2. At the end of my life on earth, my body will _____.

3. Like Job, I am certain that I will see _____ in _____.

4. I am certain of my _____.
(Answers to these questions are found on page 89)

But what will heaven be like? I am blessed. God's Word gives me a picture of heaven. It will be a place of great joy. Jesus himself tells the apostle John in the book of Revelation what it will be like for believers in heaven, "Never again will they be hungry. Never again will they be thirsty. The sun will not beat down on them. The heat of the desert will not harm them. The Lamb (Jesus) who is in the center of the area around the throne, will be their shepherd. He will lead them to springs of living water. And God will wipe away every tear from their eyes" (Revelation 7:16,17). Heaven is a place where I will be with Jesus. Heaven is a place without suffering. Heaven is a place of great happiness.

5. Heaven is a place where I will be with _____.

6. Heaven is a place without _____.

7. Heaven is a place of great _____.
(Answers to these questions are found on page 89)

Jesus gives me a picture of heaven when he tells the apostle John about who will be in heaven. He says, "After this I (John) looked and there in front of me was a huge crowd of people. They stood in front of the throne and in front of the Lamb (Jesus). There were so many that no one could count them. They came from every nation, tribe, people and language" (Revelation 7:9). How happy I am! I know that a great number of people from all over the world, young and old, rich and poor, black, white, red, brown, and yellow will be in heaven. The preaching, teaching and reading of God's Word leads countless numbers of people from every nation, tribe, and language to believe in Jesus. They will be in heaven with me.

8. There were so many people in heaven that no one could _____ them.

9. The preaching, teaching and reading of God's _____ leads countless numbers of people from every nation, tribe and language to come to _____ in Jesus.

(Answers to these questions are found on page 89)

Then Jesus reveals why they are in heaven. "They were wearing white robes... Then one of the elders spoke to me (John). 'Who are these people dressed in white robes?' he asked, 'Where did they come from?'... I answered, 'Sir, you know.' He said, 'They have washed their robes and made them white in the blood of the Lamb'" (Revelation 7:9,13,14). When I go to heaven, I will be wearing a white robe. This robe, the Bible tells us, is washed white in the blood of Jesus. "The blood of Jesus, his (God's) Son, makes me pure from all sin" (1 John 1:7). In other words, my sins are forgiven because of what Jesus did for me. Jesus covers my sinful life with a covering of his righteousness so that God does not see my sin, but rather the righteousness of Jesus. It is like snow that covers all the scars of the world and shines brightly in my eyes on a cold winter morning.

10. When I go to heaven, I will be wearing a _____ robe.

11. This robe was washed in the _____ of Jesus.

12. Jesus covers my _____ life with a covering of his _____.

13. God does not see my _____, but rather the _____ of Jesus.

(Answers to these questions are found on page 89)

There will be many people in heaven. They will stand before God's throne with their sins covered by the righteousness of Jesus. And they will sing their praises to God. "They (the people in heaven) cried out in a loud voice, 'Salvation belongs to our God, who sits on the throne. Salvation also belongs to the Lamb.' All the angels were standing around the throne... They fell down on their faces in front of the throne and worshiped God. They said, 'Amen. May praise and glory and wisdom be given to our God forever and ever. Give him thanks and honor and power and strength. Amen'" (Revelation 7:10-12). I like to sing, but the songs of praise to God in heaven will be beautiful, thoughtful, and powerful hymns of praise. They will be heard throughout all eternity.

14. The people in heaven will sing their _____ to God.

15. These hymns of praise will be heard throughout all _____.

(Answers to these questions are found on page 89)

Therefore, in thanks to God for what he has done for me, I want to serve God in my life until the day he takes me to heaven. I am blessed through God's Word, and now I want to share that Word of God with others still living in the world. I want them to know their sins are forgiven and that they can go to heaven. Jesus himself wants me to do this. Two times, after he rose from the dead and before he returned to heaven, he told his disciples and me and you to share the gospel with other people. On one occasion, on a mountain in Galilee he said, "You must go and make disciples of all nations. Baptize them... Teach them" (Matthew 28:19-20). And then again, shortly before he returned to heaven, he said, "You will be my witnesses in

Jerusalem, ... in all Judea and Samaria, ... from one end of the earth to the other" (Acts 1:8).

16. I want to serve _____ in my life until the day he takes me to _____.

17. I want to share the _____ of _____ with others still living in the world.

18. I want people to know their sins are _____ and that they can go to _____.

(Answers to these questions are found on page 89)

What a wonderful task Jesus has given me and every believer. He wants me to tell people in my family, in my village or city, in my country, yes, everyone I can in the entire world that we are saved by the grace of God, through faith in Jesus Christ. I want to tell them so that they also can be children of God and members of God's family. I want to tell them so that all the joys and peace of heaven can be theirs just as they are mine.

19. I am asked to tell people that I am saved by the _____ of God, through _____ in Jesus Christ.

20. I want to tell people that all the _____ and _____ of heaven can be theirs.

(Answers to these questions are found on page 89)

I am blessed through God's Word.

- I know Jesus lives and I also will rise from the dead on the Last Day.
- I am certain that my sins are forgiven because of what Jesus did for me.
- I am certain that I will see Jesus in heaven because of his love for me.
- I learn heaven will be a place of great joy with no more suffering.
- I learn that there will be people from all over the world in heaven.
- I and all other believers will have our sins covered by the white robe of Jesus' righteousness.
- I and all other believers will sing songs of praise to God through all eternity.
- I now want to share God's love for me with other people living in the world.
- I now want people to know that their sins are forgiven and they, too, can live in heaven.

- I now want to tell people they are saved by the grace of God through faith in Jesus Christ.

Praise God, from whom all blessings flow;
Praise him, all creatures here below;
Praise him above, ye heavenly host;
Praise Father, Son, and Holy Ghost! (CW 334)

Review of Chapter Six

Three days after Jesus died on the cross, God raised him from the dead on the day we call Easter Sunday. For the next 40 days Jesus appeared to his disciples and many other people. During those days Jesus gave these people the command to go to other people throughout the world and bring to them the good news of their salvation. Then Jesus returned to heaven.

Because Jesus rose from the dead and went to heaven, I am also certain I will rise from the dead and return to heaven both with my body and my soul. I am certain of going to heaven because God's Word tells me this will happen. I am certain of my salvation because of what Jesus did for me. I will be in heaven with him.

God's Word gives me a picture of heaven. In heaven all the sufferings and problems of life on earth, because of my sins, will be gone. I will not be the only one in heaven. A great number of people from every nation, tribe, and language will be in heaven with me. They stand before the throne of God and Jesus. They all will be in heaven because they are wearing the white robe of Jesus' righteousness. God does not look at my sin but at the righteousness of Jesus. All those who believe in Jesus will be in heaven, and they will sing their praises to God for sending Jesus to be their Savior.

From the Bible I learn all about heaven and what God has done for me through Jesus. I will share the message of the Bible in my life on earth so other people can also go to heaven to live with Jesus. I want to tell them so that all the joys and peace of heaven can be theirs just as it is mine.

Answers to the questions in Chapter Six:
1. Easter; 2. die; 3. Jesus, heaven; 4. salvation; 5. Jesus;
6. suffering; 7. joy; 8. count; 9. Word, faith; 10. white; 11. blood;
12. sinful; righteousness; 13. sin, righteousness; 14. praises;
15. eternity; 16. God, heaven; 17. Word, God; 18. forgiven, heaven; 19. grace, faith; 20. joys, peace.

Chapter Six Test

1. I am certain of my _____.

2. Heaven is a place where I will be with _____.

3. Preaching, teaching and reading of God's _____ leads countless numbers of people from every nation, tribe and language to come to _____ in Jesus.

4. Jesus covers my _____ life with a covering of his _____.

5. People in heaven will sing their _____ to God.

6. I am asked to tell people that I am saved by the _____ of God, through _____ in Jesus Christ.

7. I want people to know their sins are _____ and that they can go to _____.

8. I want to share the _____ of _____ with other people still living in the world.

(Answers to these questions are found on page 97)

God's Word tells me about rising from the dead and living in heaven:

John 11:17-27 – Jesus speaks to Martha about my rising from death.

Romans 8:38–39 – Nothing can separate me from Jesus.

Revelation 22:1-21 – Jesus gives me another picture of heaven.

John 14:1-6 – Jesus is my only way to heaven.

Word List

(A list of words you may not know or understand)

ancestor Any person living long ago from whom another person is born

assure To make something certain; to give confidence to someone

brag To praise oneself; to boast

conceiv(ed) To become pregnant with a child

commit To do something wrong, sinful, unlawful; to bind as by a promise

deceive To trick someone into believing what is false or bad

deeds Something that is done on purpose (it can be good or bad)

descendant A person who is born from a father or mother or previously born person

deserve	To be worthy of or suitable for something
exalt(s)	To make higher in rank
example	An event that is a pattern to follow
forfeit	To give up something as a penalty for something done wrong
humble(d)	Not proud; lowly; to lower the position of oneself
inherit	To receive money or something else left by someone who has died
inspire(d)	To breath into
occasion	The time of an event; a special event
pauper	A very poor person
prostitute	A person who performs sexual acts with others for pay
rebel(ed)	To fight against someone who is in authority

remedy	To correct or to make something right
response	An answer or reply
resurrection	In Christian belief, the rising of Jesus from the grave
revolt	To fight against those in power
robe	A long loose garment like a coat
sacrificial	To offer up something very valuable for someone
sermon	A talk on a religious subject usually by a pastor
stole (steal)	To take what belongs to another person without any right or permission
task	A piece of work that needs to be done
tempt	To try to persuade someone to do something sinful

temptation The act of tempting or of being tempted

trials Being tried by suffering or temptation

virgin A person without sexual experience; fresh; unspoiled

Answers to Chapter Tests

Chapter One: (page 12)
1. God's; 2. speaks; 3. all; 4. perfectly; 5. law; 6. sins, cross; 7. Savior; 8. read and study the Bible, worship Jesus in church.

Chapter Two: (pages 26-27)
1. good, evil; 2. die; 3. Satan, devil; 4. disobeyed; 5. every; 6. inherited, original; 7. death; 8. flesh, people, devil; 9. perfectly; 10. Word.

Chapter Three: (page 40)
1. Savior, Adam, Eve; 2. Mary, Bethlehem; 3. love, law; 4. sin; 5. cross; 6. grace; 7. saved; 8. faith.

Chapter Four: (page 59-60)
1. blessing; 2. man, woman; 3. God's Word; 4. ask, thank, praise; 5. holy; 6. gladly; 7. obey; 8. taxes; 9. help; 10. peace; 11. peace.

Chapter Five: (page 74-75)
1. sufferings; 2. various answers; 3. help; 4. Old Testament; 5. heaven; 6. prayed; 7. not; 8. strength; 9. us; 10. sins, forgiven, heaven.

Chapter Six: (page 90-91)
1. salvation; 2. Jesus; 3. Word, faith; 4. sinful, righteousness; 5. praises; 6. grace, faith; 7. forgiven, heaven; 8. Word, God.

Final Test

Congratulations! You have completed your study of *I am Blessed through God's Word*. Go back through the book and review any mistakes you made in the chapter tests. Also review the goals of each chapter. When you are confident or sure you know all the goals, you are ready to take the final test.

Complete the final test without looking at the text of the book. When you finish, give the test to the person who gave you the book or send it to the address found on the back cover. You may also ask for more Bible Teaching Series books to study.

If you are ready, take the test without looking back into the book.

I am Blessed through God's Word
Final Test

Fill in the blanks:

1. The Bible is _____ Word.

2. The Bible is written for _____ people.

3. I cannot keep God's law _____.

4. Jesus, as the sinless Son of God, kept God's _____ for me.

5. Jesus also was punished for my _____ when he died on the _____.

6. Jesus is my _____.

7. The leader of the evil angels is _____ also called the _____.

8. The pay I get for sin is _____.

9. Jesus overcame the temptations of the devil by using the _____ of God.

10. God promised to send a _____ to our first parents _____ and _____.

11. God sent his only Son, Jesus, born of the virgin _____ in the town of _____.

12. God's undeserved love is called _____.

13. God even gives me _____ to believe in Jesus my Savior.

14. A loving family is a _____ from God.

15. A true God pleasing marriage is one between a _____ and _____.

16. God reminds me in the Ten Commandments that I should "Remember the Sabbath day (day of rest) by keeping it _____."

17. As a citizen of my country I should _____ the government.

18. What should I do when someone needs help? I should _____ him.

19. Through faith in Jesus, I am at _____ with God.

20. I am certain of my _____.

21. Heaven is a place where I will be with _____.

22. Jesus covers my _____ life with a covering of his _____.

23. People in heaven will sing their _____ to God.

24. I want to tell people that I am saved by the _____ of God, through _____ in Jesus Christ.

25. I want to share the _____ of _____ with other people still living in the world.

Please PRINT the following information.

NAME

_____

_____

ADDRESS

_____

_____

_____

_____

Please give us your comments on this course.

_____
_____
_____
_____
_____
_____
_____
_____
_____
_____